S0-BFB-960

"A fantastic and beautiful story."
—*Seattle Times*

THE
ACORN PEOPLE

"This true story of how those dying youngsters became mountain climbers, pirates and kings is uncomfortably moving, yet told in surprisingly unsentimental terms ... Succinct and tender, it will haunt the reader long after the brief passages have been read."

—*Houston Chronicle*

"It will give your innards a bear hug. If you have ever loved a handicapped child, either personally or professionally, I promise you that you will read this story with a lump in your throat."

—*Lincoln* (Nebraska) *Journal*

"Ron Jones' true story of a group of handicapped children at summer camp is one of the most poignant, beautiful and eloquent tales to come this way in a long time."

—*Flint* (Michigan) *Journal*

Bantam Books by Ron Jones

THE ACORN PEOPLE
SAY RAY

the acorn people

Ron Jones

Illustrated by Tom Parker

BANTAM BOOKS
TORONTO · NEW YORK · LONDON · SYDNEY · AUCKLAND

RL 7, IL age 12 and up

THE ACORN PEOPLE

*A Bantam Book / published by arrangement
with the author*

Portions of this book previously appeared in
Psychology Today *and* CoEvolution Quarterly

*Bantam edition / October 1977
12 printings through February 1988*

*All rights reserved.
Copyright © 1976 by Ron Jones.
No part of this book may be reproduced or transmitted
in any form or by any means, electronic or mechanical,
including photocopying, recording, or by any information
storage and retrieval system, without permission in
writing from the publisher.
For information address: Bantam Books.*

ISBN 0-553-27385-X

Published simultaneously in the United States and Canada

Bantam Books are published by Bantam Books, a division of Bantam
Doubleday Dell Publishing Group, Inc. Its trademark, consisting of the
words "Bantam Books" and the portrayal of a rooster, is Registered
in U.S. Patent and Trademark Office and in other countries. Marca
Registrada. Bantam Books, 666 Fifth Avenue, New York, New York 10103.

PRINTED IN THE UNITED STATES OF AMERICA

O   21 20 19 18 17 16 15 14 13 12

dedication

This story is dedicated to Hilary Lael Jones, age 4, who reminded me in the midst of this work that, "You can't walk fast and eat an ice cream cone."

thankyou's

Thank you Jeremy Hewes and Willinda McCrea for editing, Sandy Clifford for the cover and design of the Zephyros edition, and Tom Parker for the illustrations.

The acorn people

day 1

Children spilled from cars and buses. It was an eerie sight. Parents carefully picked children from their perches and placed them in wheelchairs. There was an open-mouthed silence. The woods and paths of Camp Wiggin were accustomed to troops of running feet and the noise of children at play. With these wheelchair children there was only silence. It was as if the woods themselves were watching the unfolding of chairs and the lifting of bodies. All life seemed to stop. In procession, the parents wheeled their children toward awaiting counselors. I was a counselor. A target of this pilgrimage. Like everyone around me, I didn't know what to say.

Oh shit. What do you say to a parade of children who move toward you only by the energy of their parents' insistence? Who move toward you with swollen heads of gargantuan proportion. With birth scars that have left the eyes without sight or the body without arms

1

and legs. Children who seem drained of expression. Pulled into convulsions by unseen strings. Pallid in color and spirit. Beings without visible life. Crumpled and stuffed into wheelchairs. Covered with blankets, to ward off not the cold, but the vision of disfigurement.

The camp nurse had given us a one-day orientation about handicapped children, but to see this mass of injury stunned the brain. There were perhaps one hundred twenty children in all. They seemed old for their age. I remember the nurse saying, "Most will not live past their teen years. It is nature's way." She described the hydrocephalic children with heads that looked like melons about to burst. And the disease of multiple sclerosis, which ate away at the muscles leaving the body without energy or movement. The children who had mongoloid faces and a distant stare. Children with an epileptic chemistry, which at any moment could jerk the body into an unconscious spasm. Children living with an unexplained polio attack that would cruelly freeze their legs in place, leaving the rest of the body and mind to wonder at the reason for this paralysis. And finally the children who entered life without vision or a hand or perhaps a face.

The transfer of children from parent to camp staff was like a precious stamp being traded by collectors. No sign of real welcome or excitement. The stamp had value but no voice. It was one more exchange. Parents, weary of the drive and the emotion of parting, didn't say much. They paused, mentioned how nice the camp looked, and said goodbye.

Counselors welcomed their new responsibility with an equal degree of decorum. There were two counselors for each cabin of five children. I shared counseling duties with Dominic Cavelli from New York. He was a tall Italian youth with a slight but strong body, deep brown eyes that told you of his concern and love for children, and a soft manner and smile that moved across his face whenever he was about to speak. He was after a career working with handicapped children, whereas I had placed myself in this position merely for the job. Oh, I rationalized about serving others and compassion for kids, but behind this mask was a simple wish to have a good-paying job for a few weeks and to enjoy summer camp life. I had been a P.E. student and athlete in college. The thought of playing with kids, swimming all day, and taking long hikes had drawn me to this place. My illusions were quickly clouded and washed away. I wasn't about to frolic with these children. We would be lucky, I thought, if we could even take a few steps together.

As the children were assembled for cabin assignments, I wondered at this mass of humanity before me. These children with hollowed-out faces and nervous twitches. What were they thinking? Did they think? Or even feel? They all looked alike. Boys and girls inseparable by a common hurt. Did they have hopes for the future? Or was life a dulling repetition of survival? Or worse, some kind of perverted game?

I didn't have time to think. There was work to do. Every movement required a tug and a pull. Just crossing the camp from assembly point to cabin took twenty minutes per child. Some could be pushed, others had to be carried or patiently guided. Dominic and I, like the other counselors, swept back and forth freighting luggage, children and the "ditty bag" that would inevitably spill to the ground.

We didn't have any experience at this task, and the camp wasn't set up

for this kind of care. Each cabin had three steps. Steps that became hurdles. You can't wheel a chair straight up a set of stairs. I tried that with one kid and spilled him head first. Everything had to be learned. The simplest task was an ordeal.

The camp was divided into two rows of cabins. Boys on one side, girls on the other. At one end of the rows stood the camp bathroom, dining hall, swimming pool and flagpole. The flagpole had a large speaker on it that barked a greeting to all campers and played songs left over from the Boy Scouts who normally inhabited the camp. In the midst of this orchestrated hello, I was silently cursing toilets that didn't have grab bars. No sooner had one kid gotten unpacked and comfortable then it was off to the bathroom. What had always been a simple and normal act became a trial. Pants had to be pulled over cumbersome braces that grabbed and pinched at anything within reach. I had never changed someone's pants, much less balanced a child on the toilet, only to be told in crying sobs that "I don't have to go now!" Back with the pants. Lifting and tugging until at last I realize I'm sitting in the wheelchair and a wet child is now sitting in my lap. (It would be humorous once, but this struggle becomes routine.) It covers every minute and every thought, grating and shredding away any pretense or possibility for even the simplest of interaction. Every move, be it brushing teeth or simply rolling over, requires assistance. I feel like a slave and resent it.

The first evening meal was something I looked forward to. At last, the chance to sit down and eat. Dominic and I got our kids down to the hall by moving in shifts. At the table the loudspeaker once again reminded us we were on foreign turf. There was a Boy Scout prayer and then food. I started eating. Then realized that half the kids couldn't feed themselves. With unshielded anger, I started pumping spoonfuls of peas and potatoes into open mouths. Any semblance of good will or sympathy was gone. My liberal do-goodism lasted one afternoon and I wanted out.

By evening I was exhausted and angry. I questioned the camp, the loudspeaker that kept us moving, and myself. I couldn't get close to the kids and didn't want to. A fear emerged in my mind that this illness surrounding me would somehow rub off. That if I touched a disfigured limb or body, I could be poisoning myself. In a nightmare I dreamed of children's legs and heads unscrewing. Parts of bodies coming off in my hands.

day 2

Morning greeted our cabin not with the warmth of the sun, but with a chilling cold and the smell of urine. Three kids had wet their beds through. A fourth had rolled over on an artificial urine bag causing it to burst. In a stupor Dominic and I began the clean up and morning runs to the bathroom. The loudspeaker hurried everyone to breakfast with a trumpet: "You gotta get up, you gotta get up. . . ." What a joke!

It was noisy at breakfast. For the first time, I felt the kids' presence as individuals. Each of them watching Dominic and me. Stealing a glimpse and then staring. Perhaps looking at us for the first time. Seeing if we would stay. It wasn't a challenge but a real question. I felt it. I looked back.

The first of our kids was Benny B. Benny was black, peanut in size. Polio had taken his legs but not his gall or heart. He was the most mobile kid at camp. One kid that Dominic and I didn't have to push or help with the toilet. He was his own man. Most kids

9

have a "thing" they do. Something special. For Benny B. it was speed. With a crash helmet pulled tightly over his head, he hunched forward in his wheelchair like a dirt-track driver in a stock car. Once snugly into position he reared back with both arms, giving the chair a rocking motion that could be thrust forward at incredible speed. He peeled rubber and was off. Hydroplaning across the dusty camp floor. Then spinning and heading back to the cabin. Finishing the dash with a "wheelie" that only he could do. The spokes on Benny's chair were decorated with stickers and reflectors. At night he was a light streaker through camp. On the back webbing of his chair was the name of this speed freak, Benny B.

Spider was another kid in our cabin. It was a funny name because Spider didn't have any legs or arms. He had stumps that stuck out from his short frame like broken branches out of a tree. Like Benny, Spider was alert and perceptive. You could tell by his eyes. Children handicapped by illness that floods the brain with fluid or strikes off oxygen at birth seem to stare without seeing. Attention seems pulled by a constantly moving magnet. Eyes seem cloudy—unable to sparkle or hold on to anything. Spider's eyes held every-thing. And what his eyes couldn't hold, his mouth tried to trap. Spider loved to talk and talk and talk. It was like being in the presence of a jukebox. The only difference was that this machine was self-operative. Spider had to be fed, but even that didn't stop him. He just talked, swallowed and talked some more.

Far less active and alert than Benny B. or Spider was Thomas Stewart. He had muscular sclerosis, the cruelest ail-ment of all. Thomas must have been fifteen or maybe sixteen. It was hard to tell. Benny B. and Spider looked and acted like the eight- and ten-year-olds they were. But Thomas—it was hard to know anything about him. All the children were light in weight but Thomas was the lightest. He weighed about 35 pounds. Picking him up was like holding a collapsible tent. He just gave way. There was no center of grav-ity. His bones seemed unconnected. In-deed, that's what the disease had done. Over eleven years it had slowly and certainly robbed Thomas of the fiber and muscle that held his body together. (I think the act of watching and feel-ing this gave Thomas an awareness of the deterioration of his own body not felt by children afflicted from birth.) Thomas had eyes that seemed like wells. They locked up secrets. His mouth was always dry—almost crusted over. Pinched tight, as if to hold out the invading air or hold in some final scream. He watched the world about him but gave nothing to it. He was sullen, hunched over in his chair, always covered by a dark blanket. Unwilling to move unless moved. Pensive, patient, and dying.

Martin was the most able-bodied child in our group. Like other blind children in camp, he had a constant smile and seemed in perpetual motion. Sitting still, he would rock forward and back. Even standing, he swayed rhythmically. I wondered what sound or unseen tide pulled at him. Martin was extremely likable and outgoing. He was about fourteen, tall and slender, with bright red hair that stuck out in every direction. In strident steps he would march across the camp grounds. I was amazed at how straight he always walked. In many ways he seemed to navigate like a ship. He could sense tree limbs and moving objects at head level. His only sensory block seemed to be at ground level. A slight indentation or tree root would cause a faltering followed by a

12

stream of cussing. It was self-cursing; not directed at the obstacle, but at himself for not "seeing" it. Martin seemed a good kid. A little older and wiser than Benny B. or Spider and more demanding of himself than Thomas Stewart or Arid.

Arid was the fifth kid under our charge. He got his nickname from his smell. It was awful. Arid or Aaron Gerwalski didn't have a bladder or the normal means to pull waste from the body. His skin was always clammy. A large, water bottle-looking bag was attached to his intestines. The bag, strapped to his leg, collected a urine waste that had to be emptied every hour. He hated his own smell as much as those around him hated it. Arid wasn't a humorous name. This condition was terrible for anyone to carry, but for a young teenager it must have been overwhelming. The smell repelled any gesture of friendship. It stalled and interrupted any conversation before it could begin.

There you have it. The kids were gutsy and maybe even the basis for lots of self-awareness, but I wasn't enamored by the prospect. I mean this wasn't the way the job description read. Maybe I could deal with one child but the thought of responding to such

13

a thunder of pain, well, I couldn't do it. I wanted to go home. To get to the beach. To run as fast as I could. Lie in the warm sun. Breathe in deep gulps of ocean air. Anything but care for this carnage. I couldn't do it. And I didn't want to try and fake it.

In our first day of activity we were assigned to the craft area in the morning and swimming in the afternoon. I contemplated getting sick or being called away to a family emergency. I also realized that I was afraid of any action. I was afraid to leave and face the thought that "I couldn't take it." And I was afraid to stay for the same reason. There was no bravery or conviction in my action. I simply decided to stay. Like Thomas Stewart, I would close off all thoughts. I would endure.

At the craft table I rounded up Benny B., got Martin to work with Spider and gave the quiet Thomas Stewart and Arid each a private work space. Dominic went to scout the pool area and determine what kind of water activities we might get into. The craft table was full of leftover Boy Scout materials and sample projects. There were whistles, hatchet holsters, Indian headdresses, and bookends made out of pine cones. I busied myself with a nut necklace. It was an act of frustration. At least it symbolized how I felt. Crazy to be here. Absolutely crazy.

Benny B. asked what I was making and I told him, "a necklace." He could see it wasn't a designated project. Spider asked what the necklace was for. And asked. And asked. Finally I blurted, "I feel a little weird being here, so I've made myself a necklace of nuts." Spider didn't stop or recoil; he just laughed, "So do we, counselor, we're all a little nutty here!" Benny added, "You might call us the nut people, yeah, that's a good name for us." I turned to Spider to tell him, "My name isn't counselor, it's Ron." He was already off with another question, "Mr. Counselor, Ron, can we make a necklace like yours?" "Sure."

When Dominic returned we had a surprise for him. His very own acorn necklace. Benny B. had raced about collecting every nut in sight. Spider told him where most of them could be found. Martin strung most of them together. Arid was delighted by the smell. Thomas Stewart by the gift. Within this brief encounter we all had this crazy nut necklace in common.

As we moved toward the pool, the other kids noticed our necklaces. Spider

15

was quick to explain the sight. "We're the Acorn People. Can't you see?" So we were dubbed and christened by our own act. Like it or not, we became the Acorn People. My fellow travelers and I were now drawn together like blood brothers. We would share a common history and fate. We would endure together.

I'm glad I stayed. The swimming pool was a new world for everyone. The water gave buoyancy and freedom to our bodies and to the pent up children in all of us. Each child was given an orange safety belt and carefully lifted into the pool. That's where the careful and restricted movement ended and the teasing, splashing, racing began. Chil-

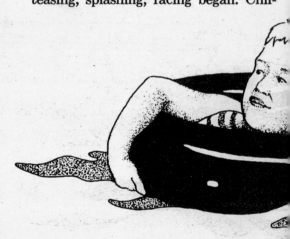

dren and counselors held in bondage to chairs and harnesses were free. It was as if the water gave us permission to push each other and not just be pushed. We were comic aliens on a strange liquid planet. Popping up and down in the water, we held each other and bobbed in unison to create huge waves. Chased about like orange speedboats. Squirted and spit at each other. Or just relaxed and let the current of play move us about. Imagined sharks and sea monsters, and pincher bugs. Yelled and screamed.

Each kid approached the water in a delightful way. Arid had to paddle about in an inner tube, holding his bag above the water. It was his secret weapon. He threatened to squirt anyone who splashed him. It was an effective threat. Benny B. grabbed a tube and—you guessed it—he became the pool's fastest inner tube. Arms flailing away like a windmill, he looked like a pool-cleaning machine gone berserk. If Benny was the speed king of the pool, Thomas Stewart was the luxury cruise ship. In elegant grace Thomas ended up sitting on three inner tubes, quietly riding the waves made by the rest of us. As for Martin, he was the classic submarine. The pressure of the water and the resonant noise of the pool seemed to give Martin a keen sense of what was happening. I watched him dodge and chase Benny B. with radar intensity. His greatest pleasure, however, was a real fright. For some reason he simply loved to unlock his belt and sink to the bottom of the pool. He would sit there cross-legged and motionless until his lungs called for breath or I reached down and grabbed him by his red hair. Thank God for that red hair. It was like a buoy that signaled for lifting. Of all the children in camp,

18

Spider was the most amazing phenomenon in water. Just as I was about to commit myself to holding him in the pool, he said he wanted to show me something. Spider could swim. I propped him up at the edge of the pool as he instructed and then waited in the water to catch him. With a head-first plunge he was in the water and pulling himself through it like a dolphin. His body seemed to lengthen out and undulate. First the head would surface, take a breath, then shoot downward, only to arc back to the surface and dive again. With this repeated whip-like motion Spider could swim. In watching Spider move with the water and use its turbulence, I thought of the fear he must have faced the first time in water and the endurance that allowed him to come to terms with this fear.

As our session in the pool ended Spider put on a demonstration of his ability by swimming the length of the pool. Several groups of children from other cabins gathered about. All watching intently this single figure submerge and surface its way across the pool. I don't think Spider had ever swum this distance. His movement in the water had slowed and almost stopped when he finally nudged the end of the pool.

When I lifted him from the water his entire face broke into a grin. There were whoops and smiles from everyone. It was not a smile I was familiar with. Not the smile of a raucous ego or aggressive threat, but the smile of knowing. The blind children show this emotion best of all. It's as if their whole face lights up. Everyone was smiling with Spider. Me too.

In our second evening of camp the Acorn Society had its first meeting. The camp loudspeaker had blared its goodnight. A lantern was our only light. It was a warm light that matched my feelings. Everyone was accounted for. Heads cranked out of sleeping bags to meet the flickering shadows. To stay in touch. A long day had passed. But we made it. I sensed that the trial was shared. It was hard on everyone. I retreated in thought, remembering how Benny had cried in the bathroom when I tried to change him. I was mad at the time; he must have been hurt and humiliated at the rough treatment I gave him. The day was full of a minutiae of events. Small victories. Just getting by was super. I felt good. I could make it. There were events like the acorn necklace and Spider's swim to keep us all going. Dominic broke into this silent thinking. We were all just looking at each other. Dominic called the meeting to order and then proceeded to tell Mafia stories. His breath danced into the cold air. I fell asleep with Mafia gangsters and gun molls running around in my mind chasing a group of kids wearing acorns around their necks.

day 3

That damned camp loudspeaker should be shot. It's warm and cozy and I don't want to get up. The floor is cold and the wheelchairs and leg braces chill the touch. Like a cavalry unit Cabin Four is getting harnessed for the day. I disconnect Aaron's bladder bag and run down to the bathroom to dump it. It's at least warm. No one has wet a bed. Yippee! I'm amazed at how quickly Dominic and I have adapted to the task of getting everyone dressed and moving. The cabin is very confining. Definitely not built for wheelchairs. For the first time I sense it and it's spoken about. We are all beginning to look forward to the day ahead. In our morning trudge to breakfast I noticed I still had on my acorn necklace. Dominic observed my discovery and pointed that he did also. So did Benny and Thomas. We all did. The Acorn People were on the move.

Camp Wiggin was administered by a retired army colonel, Mr. Bradshaw. He had a ruddy complexion and a man-

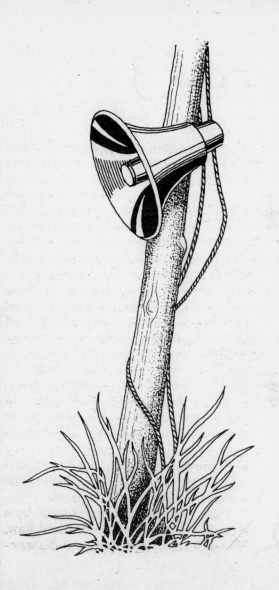

ner that matched. He administered the camp like a mandarin war lord. One day he would be at breakfast reading orders and "thoughts for the camper" and the next day he would be gone. The following day he would swoop into camp with visiting dignitaries, give another set of directives, and be off again. What he left in his wake was a set of regulations and schedules that were hand-me-downs from the scouts. They might have made sense to a group of troopers who could move between the craft center and the pool in five minutes. For us, each move was a campaign. Just getting to the pool took half an hour, with another half hour to get out of clothing and ready for the water. The recreational schedule of the camp was laid out in hourly blocks. It went something like this: Breakfast, 8:00; Crafts, 9:00; Hiking, 10:00; Study in the meadow, 11:00; Lunch, 12:00; Open recreation, 1:00; Swimming, 2:00; Dinner, 4:00; Campfire, 6:00; Taps, 7:30. It was a masterful plan, for scoutmasters. For us, it was out of the question. Each group of three cabins would rotate about the camp on its own schedule. It was like a merry-go-round. We were always moving, getting ready to move, or finishing a move. Out of the corner of our eyes we could see everyone else engaged in a similar pursuit. Besides the obvious problem of never having enough time to really do anything, this carousel schedule kept the kids from meeting other kids. You were always with the same group. This meant boys and girls were never together. Oh, perhaps that was the reason behind all this. Dominic and I decided at breakfast to talk with the kids about the day ahead as if we could plan it ourselves. Following breakfast we would go directly to the pool. The decision was unanimous.

The pool was being used by a group of girls. I could see the headlines. "Group of boys wearing nothing but acorn necklaces attacks girls in the camp pool!" That's not quite the way it happened. Participants in this first-ever "integrated swim" were self-conscious and then flirtatious in a typically pubescent way. The boys worried about their trunks being tightly tied. And their hair. My God, I had to comb their hair before they would venture out to poolside. The boys kept to one side of the pool. The girls attached themselves to the other like a string of pearls. Soon, like melting ice cream, the sun and water worked their magic. Children—

no, young adults, no, children—were playing the games of dunk and run or just plain show-off. With coy glances and gossipy chatter the girls attracted the boys' attention. The boys relied on stunts of bravery to claim equal attention. Even Thomas Stewart, the most distant of all, putted about the pool in his barge of tubes and orange jackets. I caught him smiling for the first time when he oh so slightly nudged a girl in an equally high pile of tubes. They were playing bumper cars in a soft but deliberate way. It was almost erotic. Bumping and touching each other through the elasticity and movement of the tubes.

All my questions about sex and the handicapped were answered in front of my gaze. If ever there was a dance of affection, with taunts and prowess and just plain sexual play, it was taking place in the splashes and noise before me. Our red-haired submarine found three girls of similar inclination and down they went. Arid was being pushed by Benny B. and a group of younger girls. They eventually made a chain of bobbing bodies that moved around and around the pool, interrupted by occasional water fights and screams of enjoyment. By the end of the hour, kids were helping and teaching each other their unique water tricks. There was a great deal of speculation as to who had a crush on whom. Spider had it all figured out. He had a mate for everyone at camp. As for himself, well, it was a toss-up between two of the women counselors. He liked older women.

Dressing took place at record speed. There was a new excitement in the air. Leaving the pool area with a cluster of children, I noticed that a blind girl named Mary was wearing an acorn necklace. She was a tall angular girl with a kind face and warm smile. She seemed to be aware of our presence as we started up the hill toward our cabin. I turned to Martin. He still had on his necklace. So did Thomas. The question of how she got the necklace slid from my mind and then back again with a rush as Arid complained, "I've lost my necklace . . . hey, can we stop so I can make another?" There was a chuckle at this revelation. Benny asked, "Where did you lose it?" Spider and Benny B. chided together, "Couldn't be you gave it to Mary . . . could it?" Arid looked slightly sick and then relieved as Martin saved the day with an idea. "Let's make a bunch of necklaces, OK?" Benny, not letting go, "Yeah, we can give them to our girlfriends." Thomas Stewart surprised us all by talking. He just didn't say much. His words were brief. "Not a bad idea."

We set about making acorn necklaces by the gross. By the end of the afternoon we had successfully cornered the acorn necklace market. There wasn't an acorn anywhere in sight. Not one. Benny wore his necklaces and he stuffed into suitcases those he couldn't wear. The others simply hung the treasure from their chairs. Throughout the days that followed they gave them to everyone. The entire camp—kids, counselors, cook and even Mrs. Nelson, the old nurse—became Acorn Society members.

day 6

The breakup of the schedule and the giving of the necklaces drew the camp together and gave us all a feeling of confidence and a penchant for adventure. One particular adventure, I shall never forget. It was the mountain. Our interest and knowledge of the hill came from the ever-present loudspeaker. One evening the normal recorded taps and Boy Scout pledge were followed by an announcement that special merit badges would be awarded to all those completing the climb to Lookout Mountain.

Benny B. picked up this errant message, "If the Boy Scouts can climb that mountain, can we?" Dominic and I exchanged glances of doubt and surprise. Our thoughts were picked up. Spider sided with Benny. Thomas was quiet. Arid didn't think it was too neat an idea. Martin just stood there, and then, with all our attention fixed on him, he started stamping his feet in an exaggerated march step. Hefting his knee high and then softly pulling his foot to the floor. Then with his whole body in movement, he pumped his arms and in mime fashion demonstrated that he was going to climb that mountain. He was marching off to Pretoria. There was nothing to do but follow.

In the morning we made plans to find and climb Lookout Mountain. Maps in the camp office gave the trail markings and location of the mountain. It was a six-mile hike round trip. We had no idea of the terrain. For supplies we took a bag of apples, some carrots, raisins, canteens of water and three kitchen knives. The knives were for protection. Like a military convoy we broke from camp at the first sign of morning. As we passed down the rows of cabins a few sleepy campers heard our clanking progress and asked where we were going. Benny was our voice, "To Lookout Mountain."

Dominic led the way pushing Spider. Next came Benny B. wheeling himself, followed by Martin pushing Arid. I took up the rear of the column pushing Thomas Stewart. We looked and sounded like a wagon train. Like the pioneers before us, our faces were pushed into silence by the unknown that lay ahead. There was little talk and a strange absence of humor. A sense of fear overwhelmed any thought of adventure. Each curve in the trail presented an obstacle. Our greatest hardship was trailside bushes and branches. They slashed against the wheels and, if we were not careful, entwined themselves like tentacles around the spokes and footrests. Forging through this undergrowth reminded me of Humphrey Bogart's voyage of the *African Queen*. The trail kept getting narrower. It went from a walkway to a path to a skinny trail. As the trail narrowed, our effort to push the chairs increased tremendously. In methodic lunges we crossed fields and cut into a dark wood. For the first time in my experience of pushing a wheelchair, I felt Thomas shift and lift his weight in an effort to ease the strain of movement. It was a slight adjustment but it meant he was pulling his body as hard as I was pushing. I strained ahead to see that Arid and Spider were equally at work, lifting their weight and pushing branches aside, using whatever energy they had to help our progress. The trail started upward. We had to turn around and pull the chairs from behind. Benny was forced to pull his

wheels and then brake with each stroke. Our movement was reduced to pull, stop. Pull, stop. Pull.

Perspiring and heaving for breath, I was haunted by the thought of going back. I just didn't want to turn around. It would be better to inch our way forever than to stop. Pull. Stop. Within this exertion my thoughts wandered. I felt the sensation of escape experienced in long-distance running. It's as if the mind detaches from the body. In flight it finds refreshment in abstract wonder. I pondered the condition in which people work at intricate tasks and behavior without knowing where they are headed. Surely that is the situation I am in. Where am I going? And why am I at the base of this mountain fighting to see the top? Is it the climb that's important? Or the summit? Can it be both? Or something else? Perhaps it's how we go down from the hill that counts. Or is it in simply enduring that we find the strength and purpose we seek?

Reaching exhaustion, Benny had to stop. He didn't say a word. Just stopped pushing. His chair slowly slid to a halt against Martin. Like a train being derailed we twisted to a halt. Chairs and bodies stacked upon each other. Without giving anyone the chance to think about our predicament Spider started talking. In a shrill and quick voice he began playing the role of expedition padre. Dramatically taking his canteen he sprinkled water on the hillside and proclaimed, "I hereby name this place Benny's Landing." Everyone looked up. Spider was still talking, "and claim this place and all its riches for the Acorn Society." He crossed himself and blessed the soil. Finding a willing audience Spider continued, "Mr. Thomas, I appoint you expedition recorder. Martin, you're expeditionary leader. You counselors, you're, let's see, you're soldiers. Benny, you're our scout." The drama gave us a chance to relax and realize our accomplishment. To look around for the first time in our journey. Feel the warmth of the day and the aroma of damp grass. We were in the rib of a small hill. The sun angled through the trees as if in search of someone. It splintered against the mass of rising moisture and cascaded to the ground. The air was heavy, full of light and flying things. We seemed surrounded by a soft but definable noise. A humming of insects on the move. Leaves turning to the sun. Seeds in flight. Morning dew evaporating and billowing upward. The ground drying and pulling tight.

Everyone seemed entranced by our discovery. Here we were, sitting in the middle of a forest with wheelchairs that had until now known only city streets and "convenience ramps." Spider again broke the concentration. "Well," he said, "what are you waiting for, Aaron? You're the exploration cook; break out the food." Spider was still talking as we took up the food, passed it around, and started eating. "We have more places to explore than this place, you know." With this moment of rest and Spider's encouragement our journey became enjoyable. We knew there were more places to meet, and with some patience we would find them. And so we started off again. Benny, pleased to have a place named after him, was thrilled that each time we halted there would be a similar honor. Sure enough, we "discovered" and marked our progress with Benny's Rock, Benny's Fall, Benny's Number 2 (in reference to a toilet break), and Benny's Vista.

By the end of the morning we had climbed steadily into the foothills toward Lookout Mountain. Spider was talking all the way. Naming birds, plants, and historic sights of interest. Thomas was keeping a mental diary, repeating points of importance to Benny and the rest of us. Arid was directing our culinary use of supplies and dreaming up delicious ice cream sodas and banana splits. Martin seemed to spread out. He swung erratically from side to side in his effort to pull Aaron. His head moved constantly as if it were an antenna tracking some wondrous delight. Spider finally ran out of things to name or count. Without hesitation he created and performed what he called the Acorn Marching Song. If you've ever heard the slave song "Mary Mac," you will have some notion of the noise we made crossing the wilderness.

After our succession of ceremonious starts and stops, we reached the final grade to the summit. We had covered over two-and-a-half miles. The final half mile looked straight up. More forbidding than the incline, however, was the deterioration of the trail. It simply stopped. The final grade was a hillside of slate rock and loose gravel. There would be no way to pull or push the chairs up this. The wheels simply spun around for lack of traction. Spider called this place "Desperation," but no one laughed. Dominic suggested, "How about us trying to carry everyone?" Thomas nixed the idea, "Not me, I'm not going up there on someone's back." Aaron had a similar plan, "I'll watch." Spider and Benny were talking wildly about a movie they saw in which climbers used ropes and things. During our deliberation Martin had moved several feet up the hill without our noticing. He called down to us, "Hey, you guys, it's easy." Martin was sitting down, facing downhill. By moving his legs under him in a squat position and then pushing back, he edged up the hill in this sitting posture. He looked like he was rowing a boat. Only instead of rowing across water he was literally rowing up the hill on his bottom. Using legs and arms in an accordion fashion, he made steady progress. Benny was delighted, "Martin, you're amazing." Spider added to the compliment, "Make sure that man gets the mountain cross." Thomas and Aaron were still doubtful. Leaving their wheelchairs was not an easy thing to do.

After a long debate and several demonstrations by Martin, we decided to make the ascent. Dominic sat against the hill and I placed Spider in his lap. Using belt buckles and safety straps from the wheelchairs I tied the two together. Dominic tried a few rows up the hill. It worked. Spider strapped to Dominic's stomach gave both of them the opportunity to look down the hill as they inched upward. It also freed Dominic's legs and arms for the hinge-like movement and balance necessary to squeeze up the hill and not slip back. Benny was next in line. He wanted to try it by himself. In a trial effort he worked his way up the hill and right out of his pants. At his insistence we tied a pillow from one of the chairs to his butt. He was ready. With his strength he just might be able to drag his body the distance. Martin and Aaron were next. Martin's confidence helped Aaron. In a sitting position Martin shaped his body and legs into a lap. I gently placed Aaron against Martin and bound them together. Thomas and I were at the end of the ladder. I sat on the ground in front of Thomas and pulled him first out of the chair and onto me. We twisted and rotated until both of us were comfortable. Then tied ourselves together.

Like a caterpillar we edged our way up the slate. The loose rock gave and slipped into pockets that could be used as footholds. Our trail looked like a smooth slide bordered by tractor-like gouges. I thought to myself how a hiker someday would discover our tracks and the Santa Cruz Mountains would have evidence of its very own Bigfoot. Martin's invention was marvelous. Who would have thought of going up hill backward, sitting on our bottoms? We moved in a syncopated rhythm. First the legs pushing against the hill, followed quickly by a push with both hands. We would stop to rest and then continue. (Observing the valley floor below us, we saw the tree line slipping beneath our vision, aware that we could now see valleys moving away from our vantage point like huge green waves.) At two o'clock, according to Spider, we reached the top of Lookout Mountain. He gently gave the mountain one of his necklaces. Not the act of a conqueror, but a friend. We had done it.

As with all accomplishments our attention shifted from the joy of lying across the peak of this mountain to another vision. The sky above us. Even Martin seemed to study the traces of clouds and the blueness of the space. It was strange, there was no jubilation. What had been the ultimate victory was now matter of fact. The sky beckoned. It gave us peace. There were seven of us lying faces up, just watching. A lonely piston-engine plane droned by. I love that distant whining sound. I don't think any of us had ever seen the sky in quite this way. The wheelchair and city life we all knew just didn't give us the chance. It was wonderful. This must be the exhilaration that drives explorers. The surprise of always finding another vista, a new thought, an unexpected strength. The comradeship of doing something together. Doing something no one else would dare. And in the end finding something as simple and ever-present as the sky.

The return trip to camp seemed half the time. We passed things we knew and places that were familiar. We knew where we were going. It was a quiet return. Our pace increased as we approached camp. Perhaps it was the idea of a waiting dinner or the chance to tell everyone about our climb. We wouldn't tell about the sky. It was our secret.

We arrived late to the dining hall. In dusty halos we tramped and rolled in. I guess all explorers expect a ticker-tape parade of some kind. Surely the world knew of our exploits. But the dining room was unexplainably quiet.

41

Thoughts tumbled into the void. Did we do something wrong? Would Mr. Bradshaw drum us out of camp? Had something happened to one of the kids? What's going on? Where is the laughter, the questioning, the noise? It's as if we had left a party of friends and returned to find another set of people engaged in a ritual we knew nothing about. We blended into the silence rather than interrupt it. Became a part of the stillness. Ate quickly without much emotion, anxious to get outside and learn what was wrong. It was like the first day of camp. I felt afraid.

It didn't take long to find out what had happened. The camp director, Mr. Bradshaw, had been "alarmed at the randomness of camp activities" and "concerned that parents visiting the camp on the following day would not find camp as it should be." To prepare the camp for Parent Visitation Day he announced strict adherence to the camp schedule. He had finished his remarks with "... We don't want to demonstrate *unruly behavior* at camp in front of our parents, now do we?"

We all knew what unruly behavior meant. Dominic had started teaching boys and girls the skills of cooking. He made up delicious meals. In fact he was

42

famous for his chopped hamburger, apple, cheese, and onion delight. It was a mixture of these ingredients rolled into a ball and covered with aluminum foil for cooking in an open fire. It was delicious but rather unruly. Especially since most of the food was swiped from the camp kitchen. Dominic began holding a late afternoon "eating club" attended regularly by forty or fifty kids. Aaron became assistant chef and apprentice. Most of these kids had never held a knife, let alone sliced a carrot. Dominic was a master at closing his eyes and trusting that determination could beat any palsy or lack of sight. He was right. Dominic's success with kids prompted other forms of unruly behavior.

Several women counselors had gotten interested in archery. They went to town and bought a set of inexpensive bows and arrows. It wasn't the safest place to be when they held their practice, but it was a thrill to watch children struggle to use their chairs and bodies as the means to hold the bow and draw an arrow. It was pure joy to watch arrows take flight following long moments of intensive effort and patience.

Another type of unruly conduct came

43

from Lenny X. Lenny was a black African. He was mean looking. His face scarred and twisted. You wouldn't dare meet him if it were not for his songs. Wherever he went he would be humming or whistling. You couldn't help but join in. Pretty soon you'd be humming the same song, catch Lenny's eye and smile. One day Lenny X. sat down in a shady place and just started singing. It was just after lunch when he started. He sat in that one place and sang until the late afternoon. By the time he finished every child and counselor had learned Lenny's songs. It was such a relief from the Boy Scout anthems and bugle calls that pounced from the camp loudspeaker. Lenny taught songs that, once started, could go on forever. Evenings at camp were blessed by these sounds. One cabin would start and others would softly join in until everyone was singing. These were the most tranquil hours I have ever experienced. Lenny considered songs a greeting. He explained to the children that in America you greet someone with "how are you?", whereas in Europe the greeting is "good day," and in China it's "have you eaten?" "The greetings of Senegal and Gambia," Lenny explained, "are like their songs—they ask 'do you have peace?' " His songs were like this greeting. They were expressions of peace.

The most unruly act of camp was perpetuated by the camp nurse, Mrs. Nelson. She was an older matronly-looking woman who had probably served as a nurse in World War II. She always wore the same dark blue dress with matching socks rolled under at the ankles. The aging process had not been kind to Mrs. Nelson. Although she walked with a quick gait that bespoke a once-spry woman, she was now quite heavy. Her face was always over-made-up with bright red lipstick and swooping eyebrows. Well, it was just this sight that caught some of the girls' attention. They started asking to see how she did it. I guess this might have been the first time in a long while that anyone noticed this labored beauty. She responded by giving impromptu lessons in makeup for the girls. For most, this must have been their first taste of rouge. All of a sudden half the girls had bright red lipstick. The next day they smelled like a field of lilacs and all showed up wearing face cream. Of course they thought they were beautiful. Mr. Bradshaw saw them as unruly.

The prospect of ending Dominic's eating club, the straight arrow archery team, Lenny's songfest, or Mrs. Nelson's beauty salon was out of the question. The children were learning, growing, and most important of all, they were happy. (I gauged my own change in these days by realizing what a benefit it was to be in this Boy Scout camp.) I walked around thanking stairs, bunk beds, and hills, because they made all of us behave a little more normally. The camp was not a place for handicapped children and the kids knew it. Camp Wiggin was a summer camp for children who could shoot arrows, cook goulash, take hikes, and sing songs. It wasn't a place for ramps, sanitized medical facilities, swimming pool rails, or activity schedules. It was a place for children and their expectations and fantasies for life.

day 7

The next morning was filled with orders. Each cabin had an assigned location. We were to display for the parents "what we do at camp." There were no protests or shouts of outrage. There were parents on the way. And you know—it was easier to follow directions. Our assignment was the craft area. Out came the headdress and bookends. According to Mr. Bradshaw, we were to make nametags. Using up a box of index cards we completed name plates for every child in camp. Dominic, Spider, and Martin went around delivering the tags. There were six boxes of blank cards still unused and plenty of time. Aaron was the first to see this and start to work. He scrawled a label for the Indian headdress. He carefully printed Indian Headdress and placed the card next to the artifact. Then he started on the bookends. Benny, Thomas, and I caught on. Each started making tags for trees, wheelchairs, drinking fountain, pool, nurse's station, leaf, rock, cabin door, toilet door, table, handicapped child. Dominic and his messengers started acting like Santa Claus delivering the tags. Placing them on everything. Within an hour every moving and stationary item had a label. Some had two. The camp looked like it was hit by a bumper-sticker blizzard. In the middle of the paper storm the parents started to arrive. Aaron wrote as fast as he could. He had a label for each car. And for the riders in each car

a label identifying the bearer as "parent" or "friend of parent."

Mr. Bradshaw was delighted by this flurry of activity. Everyone was busy. Everyone had a tag. The camp was a model of efficiency and order. That evening he presented the parents and campers with a treat. Following dinner we were invited to watch a film. As the light struck against the dining room wall, I couldn't believe what Mr. Bradshaw called a treat. The film dealt with water safety. There were extensive scenes about mouth-to-mouth resuscitation and how to throw a drowning swimmer a life ring. Behind the scene was the sight of children cavorting in the water. White teeth glistening. Children running and jumping into the water. I hated these blonde-headed kids and their smugness. The film ended with a Red Cross demonstration of water ballet. Graceful legs poising above the water then darting beneath its surface. Children kicking in unison toward the center of the pool to form symmetrical stars and flowers with their arms and legs. The film ended without applause.

That evening camp was quiet. There was no singing. Dominic didn't tell any Mafia epics. And those labels were like

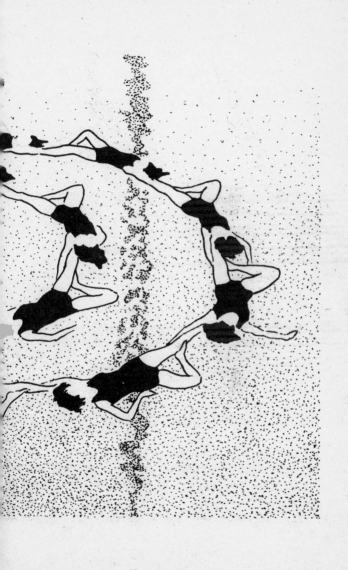

a hundred spying eyes. They were
everywhere. Reminders of who we were
and what our place was in the order
of things. Late into the night I was
awakened by a crash of ash cans and
an erratic flashlight that shot right into
my face. In a stupor I climbed out of
bed and headed toward the noise. I
thought one of the kids had gotten
tangled up trying to go to the bathroom. The noise of crashing and thrash-
ing about increased as I got closer. It
was Mrs. Nelson; she was lying on the
ground with this big smile and one up-
raised eye. Her flashlight swinging
wildly. She was totally inebriated. No,
she was blind drunk. In her hand she
had a dozen or so labels. She threw her
head back and in a slur of perfection
declared, "See here, I've got them . . .
all of them." "Well, not quite," I
thought, "but you've got the idea." I
picked her up and we weaved together
through the camp toward her cabin.
Along the way she would sway to rip
off a label here and a label there. I
started helping her in this purge. She
smiled and giggled at the sight of help.
Together we did the deed.

day 8

Next morning everyone asked who had removed the labels. Even Mr. Bradshaw was missing. He was off on another fund-raising junket. There was speculation that the good camp fairy had made the visit. Spider was convinced it was the Green Hornet! Aaron voted for Mr. Clean. Martin speculated that bears did it. The questioning and hypotheses about our benefactor raged between breakfast cereal, fruit, and rolls. It's funny how heroes must always be bigger than life.

Like the surprise and wonder of finding the sky, revolution can't be planned. It happens when you least expect it. Its clerics are not bigger than life but humble and simple souls. Like the person next to you. Revolution is a Rosa Parks, who decides one day not to ride in the back of the bus. Or a navy nurse named Mrs. Nelson, who suddenly refuses to let her children be condemned to a label.

Throughout the hubbub Mrs. Nelson sat in a corner holding her head and nursing a cup of coffee. As curiosity crescendoed I informed these seekers of the truth that "I know who did it!" It was a pleasure to know that although I couldn't act like a rebel, I at least could identify one if the chance presented itself. The time was now. I pointed deliberately to the corner of the room. Everyone looked and then looked back. "So who did it?" Spider inquired. I pointed again. "Not Mrs. Nelson," chided Benny. "Yes, Mrs. Nelson," I replied.

Mrs. Nelson was a genuine camp hero. It couldn't have happened to a nicer person. I'm not at all sure she remembered her gallantry but her legend spread unabated. From that moment she couldn't keep the kids away from her. You might say she was captured by good intentions. Kids would huddle around her proposing things to do. It was as if she possessed some kind of magic. Well, maybe she did. After all, she stripped those labels off all of us. She gave us back the chance to be children. To dream and play.

day 10

Play we did. Some of the girls organized a dance. It was crazy. Beautiful. We all dressed up. The boys perfumed themselves with Wildroot and Dixie Peach. Martin got his rangy red hair into a ducktail. Benny and Thomas settled for the natural look. Spider had his hair slicked into a Rudy Vallee shine. Aaron had a crew cut that with the aid of Vaseline stood straight up. All three inches of it. The girls wore pony tails and lots of ribbons. For music we had Mrs. Nelson's slow records. Can you believe Frank Sinatra? For those into the twist we had the Chantells or some such group. We also had some down home country music and one record of the bunny hop. The dance started like every dance. Boys on one side of the dining hall, girls facing them. Three records played and no one moved. Janie, one of the girl counselors, took the hands of some of the blind girls and made a line. She started describing out loud what she was doing. There was a great squeal of "oh no's."

Janie walked over to the record machine and put on her favorite country song. Back she sashayed to the waiting line of girls, broke into the middle of the line and shouted, "Here we go! Four steps forward. Four steps back. Turn around and slap your back." She was giving a spontaneous square dance call. I grabbed Martin and some kids in chairs and we followed Janie's call. Circled right. Turned around and said goodnight. Pretty soon the whole hall of kids and counselors was moving to Janie's call. Not all together mind you. But moving. We were the dancingest moving fools you ever saw.

Once you start it's hard to stop. Janie called a Virginia Reel. She had the boys line up across from the girls, then peel off in couples and parade, wiggle or wheel down the corridor of clapping, shouting kids. There was a commotion of jockeying to line up with the right partner. With our kids the chance to dance with a girl brought a mixed and surprising reaction. Benny B. would have nothing to do with this nonsense. He sped about the hall showing off to a diminishing audience. Martin had the dilemma of three girlfriends. They were his diving friends at the pool. He asked if he could "cut in" on the line so that he would have the chance to, as he put it, "share himself with the ladies." I promised to help him. Aaron, of course, had to dance with Mary. Thomas wanted to watch. Spider was courting his favorite girl counselor.

I don't think you could call what we did a classic Virginia Reel. What took place reminded me of kids on "Bandstand" doing that jive stroll as others stood applauding and moving up the line for their turn. For our kids the slightest turn of the shoulder or turn of the wheelchair was rewarded. Every dancer had his own style. They slipped, slid and just had fun. By the end of the dance the kids and counselors were making up their own rules. Groups of four or five children and counselors would grab hands and come down the center of clapping contestants. Martin was last down. He had the biggest grin on his face I've ever seen. He also had three young ladies.

If the stroll was for the big kids, the bunny hop was for the kid in all of us. Everyone could do it. This was Benny's favorite. We formed a big conga line of wheelchairs and weaving bodies. With a hop hop hop or its equivalent the Bunny Hop began. Closing your eyes and listening to the screams of delight and exhilaration you might imagine yourself in the heart of the old fun house at the beach in San Francisco.

Finally the big moment of the dance arrived. Janie asked for quiet. Then, with everyone at attention, she announced the crowning of the Camp Wiggin King and Queen. I knew it. I knew those girls would romanticize this occasion. No dance is proper without such goo. Benny and I were allies on this. Benny complained, "Oh heavens no." I agreed. Spider in typical good humor suggested in undertone, "Mr. Bradshaw for king." Like most King and Queen things I knew it was fixed. I knew who would reign.

I was wrong again. Mrs. Nelson was a perfect Queen. She preened and threw kisses to everyone. So who would be King? There was the traditional murmur and rustle. "The girl counselors, after consulting with girl campers, and the camp cook, proudly and with great honor proclaim the next King of Camp Wiggin to be . . . Aaron Gerwalski." "Who?" "Aaron Gerwalski." "That's Arid." "It's our Aaron." Even Benny was excited. "Our man Arid did it, he made it," he said. "Yeah, and he gets to kiss all the girls," added

Spider. Aaron was a perfect choice. In grand style we wheeled him to his waiting throne and his Queen. She picked him up and gave him a big kiss. Bright red lipstick right on the forehead. Aaron was speechless, embarrassed, and thrilled all at once. Buffeted by all this attention. Searching for a reason for this adulation, he turned to the assembly and before he could speak answers began to break their way toward him. "It's your hair, it can hold a crown by sticking to it." "Aaron, you're the best cook in camp." "Aaron, you're just neat." That last comment caught Aaron's need. He turned and smiled in the direction of the comment. His expression ignited the crowd into three cheers. Three cheers for the King and Queen of Camp Wiggin.

It's not easy being a king one moment and a child the next. Wheeling Aaron back to our cabin I couldn't see his face for the evening shadows. I could feel his body in the chair. He had his hands cupped over his face. He bent forward in his chair. Body shaking and quivering. Taking in quick gulps of air. Then pushing the air out in repeated sobs. Tears were streaming down his face as he turned in embarrassment from other campers. "I've never been a

59

king before." Still pushing him slowly I responded, "Most of us will never be kings." Aaron continued, "But I'm so happy, why am I crying?" Before I could think of an answer he had another question. "Do kings cry?" I had an answer, "Yes."

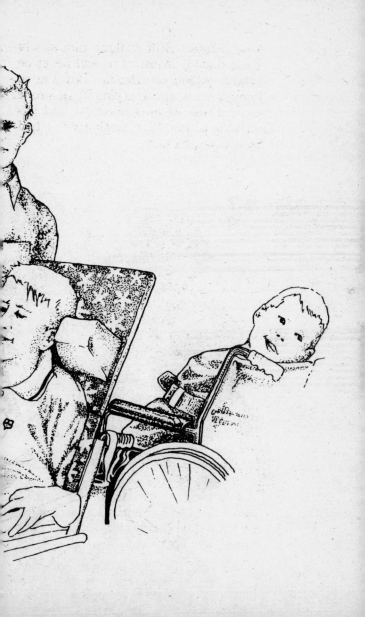

That night camp filled with the shepherd chorus of Cum Ba Ya. One cabin would start singing. Others would join in and then silently hold their voices and just listen to the others singing. We were at peace with the world. I thought I could hear each voice in the camp somehow held suspended by all the voices. And the soft singing of Benny and Spider. And what a marvel —Thomas singing faintly for the first time.

Someone's singing, my Lord
Cum Ba Ya
Someone's praying, my Lord
Cum Ba Ya
Someone's singing, my Lord
Cum Ba Ya
Oh, Lord
Come By Here.

Why can't life be like this? Human beings in all their magnificence. Working to find that moment of pride. That one second of excellence at being alive. Hearing our singular voice held in harmony by the voices of those we love. The feeling of belonging not just to oneself but to the entire universe.

Camp days fled by like a tide leaving the sand. Each day seemed shorter.

62

There were signs of anxiety. "How many days left?" was a constant question. The kids seemed to withdraw gradually but perceptibly into cocoons. I noticed that Thomas stopped talking and was slumping in his chair. Benny B. was racing about in a frantic way. He told me that if he stopped the camp would end. The closing date was looming larger and larger. Mr. Bradshaw returned to camp to remind us that parents would arrive to be with us all day the upcoming Saturday. And final camp activities would end Saturday afternoon. He wanted the camp clean. So that was our fate. To spend the last three days of camp cleaning and waiting. I was asked to clean the pool. The place that we enjoyed the most was to sit unused.

Mrs. Nelson felt the brunt of this depression. Most of the girls returned their makeup and many children displayed symptoms of illness that marked their first few days at camp. Bedwetting returned. Those kids on special diets who had been eating regular meals or Dominic's concoctions requested their pills again and wanted pampering. Mr. Bradshaw provided the final blow to morale when he informed us that he planned another water film for Saturday. There was no response to this suggestion. In desperation I asked if we could at least keep the pool open until Saturday so that we could demonstrate how many of the kids had learned to swim. "Mr. Jones," he said, looking right at me, "the pool is your responsibility. Just be sure it's clean by the closing of the camp on Saturday." There was still no reaction from the kids. Mr. Bradshaw left the room and the camp. In leaving he thanked and complimented us for being good campers and counselors. He was proud to be a part of Camp Wiggin. And knew the parents would be pleased on Saturday. No one moved.

3 days to go

We sat in silence for what seemed like an hour. Finally Mrs. Nelson started walking around the room with her hands behind her back like a priest on a morning walk. We all watched her circle quietly and then come to a sudden stop. "Why don't we . . ." she said. "Why don't we put on our own water ballet? Put on an extravaganza. With costumes. And a story. Everyone can take part. We'll put on a show for the parents. Well, what about it? Do we sit on our duffs feeling sorry for ourselves or do we do something? I'll get reporters and they can film us . . ."

That did it. That was the trigger. Film. Reporters. These kids had never been news. Most had been family secrets. They had been observers. Now they had the chance to be performers. "Can we do it?" someone asked, and before anyone could answer there was a resounding "We can."

2 days to go

We had two days to prepare for the Camp Wiggin Water Extravaganza. Mrs. Nelson came to the pool for the first time. She had on an old wrinkled bathing suit and white skin that piled about her. She was a brave lady. I don't honestly think she could swim. Armed with ignorance, a drill-sergeant voice, and lots of courage, she started directing what she called *The Acorn Pirate*. She had in her hands several pieces of paper that looked like a diagram for building the great pyramid.

With Mrs. Nelson's directions, materials from the craft center, and lots of work, the pool was transformed into a lagoon complete with pirate ship, palm tree, and exotic plants. And, oh yes, one native idol. The changing rooms at the end of the pool were painted to look like the side of a ship. Portholes replaced windows. The flagpole with its speaker became the mast of the ship U.S.S. Acorn. Probably the first pirate ship commissioned into the navy by an ex-navy nurse. A sail was fashioned out of sheets, and a jolly roger pennant was fitted out slightly below Old Glory. Next came the costumes. The inner tubes were made into floating islands of flowers. Safety belts became ballet skirts, pirate belts, and native war dress. *South Pacific*, look out!

1 day left

With one day left we had our set. It looked beautiful, this rogue pirate ship setting in the middle of Camp Wiggin. Now for the performance. Mrs. Nelson called everyone together. She divided us into pirates and natives. Good guys and bad. As for the script itself, well, that seemed still to be a mystery. Once into our roles we were given various options. We could be divers. Or racers. Or dancers. We practiced our separate parts. The divers sinking to the bottom of the pool, on cue, of course. The racers pushing their inner tubes across the pool in intricate patterns. The dancers practicing a kind of T'ai-Chi on the pool deck.

O days left

Saturday was the big day. The Camp Wiggin Water Extravaganza was about to begin. Everyone went right to the pool to hear Mrs. Nelson's final instructions and get into their costumes. Mrs. Nelson began talking, "Now children, I'll read the story over the camp loudspeaker. All you have to do is listen carefully and follow my instructions." As if on cue, cars loaded with parents, brothers, and sisters of the campers started arriving. They parked and were immediately greeted by a welcome committee that plied them with a flower lei and invited them to the pool area for a play to be performed by the campers and staff. Janie and some of the girl counselors had ridden into Santa Cruz the evening before and to everyone's enjoyment returned with boxes full of begonias. They worked all evening making leis. The surplus flowers covered the pool in bright exotic colors.

Parents conditioned to strained greetings were delighted. Family children accustomed to pampering or resenting their handicapped brother or sister found themselves wishing to be in the play. You could see smiles flash across the faces of the hosts. Pirates and natives waved to their bemused families. The excited and curious audience was directed to take seats around the pool. Mr. Bradshaw was late to arrive. With a delegation of trustees behind him, he faced a play about to begin. There was only one thing to do. Join in like everyone else. Well, at least the pool was clean. It even had flowers.

Mrs. Nelson approached the microphone. Papers in hand, she started to narrate and direct our water epic. "Once upon a time, an ugly pirate—that's you, Mr. Jones—sailed his ship the U.S.S. Acorn in Camp Wiggin Lagoon. The pirates with Mr. Jones were a villainous lot. Well, look mean, you pirates. That's right. Stomp around. Show off your eye patches and swórds. Shake your fists at the natives. Good."

"The peaceful natives of the lagoon were a powerful and beautiful people. They simply chided (that's make faces) and taunted the pirates."

"The pirates, angered at this show of disrespect, pointed to their skull-and-cross-bone flag. Finally, the captain of the pirates stepped out on the gang-plank. That's the diving board, Mr. Jones. (No one said pirates were smart.) The captain of the pirates, a ferocious braggart, declared that he came for the treasure in the lagoon and that nothing would stop him. To get the treasure, he challenged the natives to a contest. It would be his pirates versus the natives. May the best group win."

Given this order to act, I pranced about looking all the natives straight in the eye. Then I walked about displaying the muscles and strength of my fellow pirates. In silent movie fashion I was overly dramatic. I know, because the audience started booing me. Imagine me, the most virile of pirates, being booed. Most of the kids got the idea and started posturing and posing. Spider and Martin played natives. When I passed each of them I lifted my eye patch and gave a pirate wink. They laughed and in retribution shook their acorn necklaces in my face. Taunting and teasing I tried to encounter each of the pirates and natives. I paused by each player to make some kind of gesture or salute, giving everyone a chance to receive some applause and recognition. The audience was fantastic. They got the idea and warmly greeted each of the players. The stage was set.

"All right, Mr. Jones, that's enough," called Mrs. Nelson. "The story must go on. And so the pirates challenged the natives to a contest of strength and wisdom. The first event of the contest was the dive for treasures."

With this introduction, Mrs. Nelson pulled a box from the girl's dressing room and with a heave dumped the contents into the pool. It was the camp silverware. Every last knife, fork and spoon. Returning to the microphone, Mrs. Nelson calmly continued her narrative chatter.

"Pirate and native divers went into the water to collect the treasure."

The divers entered the pool. There were the sinkers like Martin, who silently submerged and in a sitting posture on the bottom used their arms and legs to scoop up the booty. And there were the divers. Those kids who went down head first tracking down a single piece of silver. Of course the audience awarded each find with hurrahs. With almost all of the treasure collected and piled on the pool side, Mrs. Nelson continued her story.

72

"The treasure was taken to the native temple of Oh La where it could receive the blessing of the god Oh La. OK, you pirates and native dancers, you heard me. The treasure was taken to the temple. That's it. Good. Now the only way the god Oh La would release the treasure was with the satisfactory performance of the legendary water ballet."

Given this signal the pirate and native players who had practiced roving about the pool were placed in their respective inner tubes. From the various edges of the pool they kicked and splashed into the center of the pool where they formed a large circle. Then with the orchestration of Mrs. Nelson the circle was pushed in a clockwise and then counter-clockwise maneuver. The audience clapped in appreciation. It was hard. Kids like Benny wanted to go fast, while kids like Aaron and Thomas were doing all they could just to keep afloat. Each had to show a great deal of tolerance.

The circle move was followed by the formation of a floating star. And then the division of floaters into two lines. It was the Virginia Reel on water. The gods must have been happy. As the

73

water ballet ended Mrs. Nelson proclaimed that a final contest would mark the end of the water extravaganza.

"With approval from the god Oh La the treasure was to be given to the winner of a race between the captain of the pirates, that's Mr. Jones, and the best native swimmer of all time—Spider, The Unconquerable."

It was obvious from the corresponding boos and adulation that Spider was the odds-on favorite. To build up for the big race, some of the pirates and I did evil-looking dives. The natives countered with their own dives. (Actually we had several kids who thought big splashes were the only appropriate act for such a play.) With the completion of the dives, the race was about to begin. Mrs. Nelson began explaining how the contest would be fought.

"According to ancient tradition Spider would be allowed to start first. This swimming start is to offset the fact that the captain of the pirates is known to cheat and use the gangplank as a diving board. Are you ready? Will someone help Spider get ready? All right. On your mark, get set, go!"

In the midst of a great roar Spider was off. Surging and kicking with all his might. I watched carefully, trying

74

to calculate when I should dive. I knew that a running dive even done with lots of wasted motion could carry me a fourth of the distance across the pool. I also knew that to Spider this was a race and it wouldn't be right not to go all out. With this in mind I gave a pirate yell and dove headlong after Spider. I came up and spotted Spider perhaps halfway down the pool. With exaggerated but sure strokes I quickly began to close the distance. I could hear the crowd yelling frantically for Spider. "Faster!" "Faster!" "Come on, Spider!"

Just a little past halfway I drew abreast of Spider. I hesitated, trying to think what to do. To roll over and back stroke. To dive under water perhaps and swim the distance out of public sight. I was now a clear body length in front of Spider.

I heard a yell. I looked over at Spider. With a jerk he was out of the water. In fact he looked like a rock skipping over the water's surface. He was alongside of me and then past me. Faster and then faster. I started swimming with all my might. Spider was cutting across the water at an incredible speed. I couldn't catch him. The crowd was ecstatic. Like a one-sided

75

tug-of-war the natives had tied a rope to Spider and in unison were now beginning to pull him down the pool. He was bouncing over the water toward the end of the pool. With all my might I couldn't reach the edge and stop this rush. Everyone was yelling. Just as Spider was about to be yanked right through the pool side, the rope went slack and he coasted to the side like a surfer on a wave. Spider had won.

The race, the summer camp, the companionships were ended. Quiet moments of goodbye. I was reminded of our first meeting. A silent exchange. Now it was taking place again. Children, the precious bond to life, were being passed from counselor back to parent. It was quiet. Benny rolled slowly by himself from our presence. Spider was passed from arm to arm. Martin walked holding my hand. He was leading. Thomas Stewart had to be carried. His eyes were a little older and sadder. Aaron wanted to push himself. Show his parents his strength and acorn necklace.

For many of the girl campers the farewell was of special significance. They had become young women. One carried a hidden crush. The word filtered to me like a breeze. Several girls broke from the goodbye with parents and hurried to the pool. I felt very embarrassed by this rendezvous. They pushed and prodded one of their members forward and then vanished. It was a close friend of Mary—the girl Aaron had given his necklace to. She was equally embarrassed yet demanding of the situation. She had enjoyed summer camp. Loved my voice and enthusiasm. Thought I was a good pirate. Wanted to know if I would write. Wanted to hold my hand. Touch my face. I held her hand very gently. She asked me if I would close my eyes. If I would be at summer camp next year. If I would say goodbye. With a kiss. I bent down and touched her lips with mine. I would be here. I would remember summer camp forever.

This unexpected moment took me away. I didn't even see the members of the Acorn Society leave. I think they knew and even approved. They understood and felt many things I would never comprehend. They were racers, mountain climbers, observers, and kings. And they were dying. "Most wouldn't live past the teen years."

epilog

All the principal children in this story are now dead. Dominic and I kept in close touch with these children for five years. Dominic's connections with the Mafia turned out to be more real than story. With money from legitimate business and lots of volunteer help, Dominic and I conducted trips for these friends and an annual Christmas party. Thomas and Aaron died one year after summer camp. Spider was killed by a car the following year. Martin died in a car accident four years later. Benny B. was the last child to leave this place. Of all the children he was the only one to have a funeral. At the final service Benny's mother gave me a white envelope. Inside was a crumpled acorn necklace. She said he gave them to everyone he met.

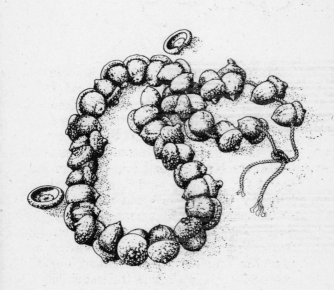

ABOUT THE AUTHOR

RON JONES has been a teacher for over 20 years, often in unusual, difficult and controversial positions that have since become the inspiration for his writing. His early experiences as a counselor at a summer camp for handicapped children are reflected in THE ACORN PEOPLE, which was made into an award-winning TV movie. Another TV movie, THE WAVE, was based on a story in his collection, NO SUBSTITUTE FOR MADNESS, about his experiments with his history class at Cubberley High School in Palo Alto. A later teaching job, in the psychiatric ward of a large city hospital, became the basis for KIDS CALLED CRAZY.

In 1972, Jones founded the Zephyros Educational Exchange, a non-profit group of parents, artists and teachers that write, print and distribute their own teaching materials. Since 1978 he has been physical education director at San Francisco's Recreation Center of the Handicapped, where he works with 1,200 physically and mentally disabled children and adults. His most recent book, SAY RAY, was drawn from his experiences there. He lives with his wife Deanna, a professional potter, and daughter Hilary in the Haight-Ashbury section of San Francisco.

STARFIRE ®

☐ **DADDY LONG LEGS**   25233/$2.50

All her life Jerusha Abbott has lived at the dreary John Grier Home for Orphans. But now she is seventeen and must face an unkind, lonely world on her own. Things turn around when suddenly an anonymous benefactor sends her to a posh Northeastern college for women, simply with the condition that she keep "Daddy Long Legs," as she's nicknamed him, aware of her progress. And what progress it is! From reading to sports to writing to earning a scholarship to falling in love, she succeeds in everything she does and learns to like herself for the first time.

☐ **THE SISTERS IMPOSSIBLE**   26013/$2.50

As sisters go, Saundra and Lily have never been the best of friends. But the real trouble starts when their father buys younger sister Lily a pair of dancing shoes so she can go to ballet school with the beautiful and accomplished Saundra. If it weren't bad enough to have her bratty sister tagging along, it's much worse when that sister befriends Saundra's worst enemy and rival, Meredith. And when Lily *must* choose between Saundra and Meredith, which will win out—sibling loyalty or rivalry?

☐ **CHEAPER BY THE DOZEN**   27250/$3.50

What do you get when you put 12 lively, red-haired, freckle-faced kids with a father who believes a family can be run as efficiently as a factory and a mother who is his partner in everything except discipline? You get an hilarious tale of growing up that has made generations of kids laugh along with the Gilbraiths. Who can forget a first date, with Dad in the back seat, or a scene where tonsils are removed en masse? Don't miss this funny and delightful story of one of America's best-loved families.

☐ BELLES ON THEIR TOES
25605/$2.95

The pleasure continues as the Gilbraiths return, a little older, a little wiser but no less delightful. The eldest of the 12 children is now 18, the youngest is two, and father has passed away. But the antics of this resourceful clan continue unabated as the family learns to pitch in and pinch pennies to make ends meet—rising to every crisis with a marvelous sense of fun. The "sincere and heartwarming atmosphere in this second volume . . . makes it almost better reading, if possible, than the first."

☐ LITTLE WOMEN
21275/$3.50

Quite simply, no young girl should grow up without reading this story of four very different young girls, and the twists and turns their lives take as they and their beloved Marmee struggle against poverty and loss with good nature and irresistible jollity. Share the laughter and tears as Meg, Jo, Beth and Amy live, love and learn with each turning page. No one can read this heartwarming saga without a fair share of laughter and tears—it is a book to read over and over with renewed pleasure each time.

Buy them at your bookstore or use this handy coupon for ordering:

Bantam Books, Inc., Dept. EDN 7, 414 East Golf Road,
Des Plaines, Ill. 60016

Please send me the books I have checked above. I am enclosing
$_____ (Please add $1.50 to cover postage and handling. Send
check or money order—no cash or C.O.D.s please).

Mr/Ms _____

Address _____

City/State _____ Zip _____

EDN7—1/88

Please allow four to six weeks for delivery. This offer expires 7/88.
Prices and availability subject to change without notice.

Shop at home
for quality children's books
and save money, too.

Now you can order books for the whole family from Bantam's latest catalog of hundreds of titles including many fine children's books. *And* this special offer gives you an opportunity to purchase a Bantam book for only 50¢. Here's how:

By ordering any five books at the regular price per order, you can also choose any other single book listed (up to a $5.95 value) for just 50¢. Some restrictions do apply, so for further details send for Bantam's catalog of titles today.

BANTAM BOOKS, INC.
P.O. Box 1006, South Holland, Ill. 60473

Mr./Mrs./Ms. _____
                                (please print)

Address _____

City _____ State _____ Zip _____
                                                       FC(C)—10/87

Printed in the U.S.A.